WORDS

KENNETH E. HAGIN

Chapter 1
TALKED TO DEATH—OR LIFE

Jesus Himself said, *"For by thy WORDS thou shalt be justified, and by thy WORDS thou shalt be condemned"* (Matt. 12:37).

When I was meditating on this subject, one word from this text kept going over and over in my spirit, and that was the word WORDS. Something on the inside of me seemed to impress me to teach on WORDS. WORDS are more important than a lot of people realize.

WORDS make us or break us.

WORDS heal us or make us sick.

According to the Bible, WORDS destroy us or make us full of life, happiness, and health.

Our WORDS—the WORDS we spoke

yesterday—made life what it is today.

That agrees with what Jesus said in Mark 11:23, *"For verily I say unto you, That whosoever shall SAY unto this mountain, Be thou removed, and be thou cast into the sea; and shall not doubt in his heart, but shall believe that those things which he SAITH shall come to pass; he shall have whatsoever he SAITH."*

You could read that like this: *"He shall have whatsoever—the WORDS—he speaks."*

In June 1943, I was starting a meeting for a Pastor A. in the East Texas oil fields. He had had a serious heart attack. One of the neighboring pastors told me, "Brother Hagin, for two or three days the doctor tried to get us to quit praying for Pastor A. He was between life and death, and the doctor said, 'You're holding him here by your prayers and faith. If he does revive—which I doubt—his mind will never be right, because blood didn't get to his brain for more than 10 minutes.'

"But we just couldn't stop praying for him," the pastor said. "We kept praying. The third day Pastor A. revived, and his mind is all right. The doctors are shocked."

Pastor A. had not resumed preaching yet. His wife, who was also a minister, was filling the pulpit. My wife and I and our children stayed in the parsonage with them, and we all went to church in one car.

One night, Pastor A. started to make an announcement, and he said it backwards. The minute he got into the car, his wife said, "You made a mess of that. It's just like the doctor said. I guess you'll have to quit preaching."

My wife spoke up and said, "There is nothing wrong with Kenneth's mind, yet he did worse than your husband. Kenneth got his tongue tangled up three times tonight."

But Pastor A.'s wife said, "You'll have to quit preaching." She was constantly telling him what he couldn't do.

One day after we ate our main meal, my wife went to the beauty shop and Pastor A. went to visit someone who was sick, so I helped Mrs. A. with the dishes. As we were standing there washing and drying the dishes, the Lord inspired me to say, "Sister A., I don't know how you'll take this, but if you don't quit talking like you do to your husband, he'll be dead in two years. You're going to talk him to death!"

Mrs. A. flared up at me, and I said, "Now, wait just a minute, Sister. Wait just a minute! You know that wasn't Kenneth Hagin who said that. The Spirit of God inspired me to tell you that. I would stake my life on it."

So she simmered down and said, "Brother Hagin, we've known you for a number of years, and we know how God uses you, so I'll accept that from the Lord."

While we were there, she did better. A year later, we were visiting them again, and she was right back to her old ways, talking death to her husband, saying, "You're going to die. You'll never make it!"

I tried to get her to stop, but she just shook her head "no" and wouldn't listen.

Then, a few months later, I was holding a revival for a friend who pastored Brother A.'s home church. And while I was in that revival, they came and preached Brother A.'s funeral. I compared notes, and it was almost exactly two years from the day that I had had that word for his wife.

After his death, Mrs. A. got angry at God

because her husband died. She never preached another sermon. She backslid, and as far as I know, their children never lived for the Lord. Thank God, the husband went to heaven.

All that happened because of WORDS.

Forty-five years ago, I was a Baptist boy lying on a bed of sickness when I received the revelation of God's Word. I began by acting on Mark 11:23, 24, saying, "I believe."

WORDS WERE SPOKEN.

I said, "I believe I receive healing for my deformed heart.

"I believe I receive healing for the incurable blood disease.

"I believe I receive healing for the paralysis.

"I believe I receive healing from the top of my head to the soles of my feet."

And within the hour, I was standing on my feet.

I had learned the secret of WORDS—FAITH WORDS.

Forty-five years have come and gone, and I haven't had a headache. Not one. The last headache I can actually remember having was in August 1933.

I haven't had a headache, and I'm not expecting to have one. But if I had a headache, I wouldn't tell anybody. And if somebody asked me how I was feeling, I would say, "I'm fine, thank you."

I would speak the right WORDS, because Jesus said in Mark 11:23, *"he shall have whatsoever he saith."* I believe what the Word of God says in Isaiah 53:5, *"with his stripes we are healed."* I believe that. I believe I am healed.

Chapter 2
HOW YOUR WORDS
AFFECT YOUR CHILDREN

When Ken Jr. was 2½ hours old, I held that little fellow up in my hands and said, "Lord, thank you for this boy. I realize that You've given this new life that I hold in my hands to my wife and me.

"I realize that it's my responsibility, because I know the Bible, to train up this child in the way he should go, and when he is old, he will not depart from it.

"I realize that Your Word says to bring children up in the nurture and admonition of the Lord, and I'm going to do it. I'm going to do it because children are trained not only by precept, but also by example. I'm going to live right in front of him. I'm going to do what's right. And I'll be honest with You if I miss it."

When our little girl, Pat, was born, I took her into my hands immediately, and said the same thing I had said over Ken: "I'll do right. I'll raise her right. I'll train her. I'll set the right example in front of her and teach her precepts from the Word of God. I will also teach her by example.

"I know you can have what you say, so I say that this child, like Ken, will grow up strong physically, without sickness or disease, will be alert mentally, and stalwart spiritually."

Years afterwards, even our kinfolk, who felt we had ruined everything by going off with tongue-talkers, said, "There is something to that. There has to be. Kenneth's children are never sick."

I never prayed in my life that either of my children would be saved. Not one single prayer. I never prayed a prayer that either one of them would be filled with the Spirit. They're adults now with families of their own and I don't believe I prayed more than half a dozen times for both of them in all these years.

Why? Because you can have what you say—

and I had already said it! If I were to pray about it now, it would mean that I didn't mean it then. They got saved and filled with the Spirit at an early age.

Sometimes I had to go to them when they were little and say, "Forgive me; Daddy acted ugly" if I lost my temper. I had to say, "I've set the wrong example. I've asked the Lord to forgive me, and He's forgiven me. Will you forgive me?"

And those little children would say, "All right."

I never told my children not to do something "just because I tell you not to." I sat down and read the Bible to them, proving to them that I had their interests at heart.

If I had to reprimand them or even spank them, I said, "It says right here in Ephesians 6, *'Children, obey your parents in the Lord: for this is right. Honour thy father and mother; (which is the first commandment with promise;) that it may be well with thee, and thou mayest live long on the earth.'* "

I explained to them that days a person is sick or in the hospital are not well days. I said,

"See, I want it to be well with you. I want you to enjoy long years on the earth."

CHILDREN ARE A PRODUCT OF WORDS.

Words heal us or make us sick.

Words bless us or curse us.

The words that I hear in the morning will linger with me all through the day.

How little wives may realize that a biting, stinging word in the morning will rob a husband of efficiency the whole day long. But a loving, tender, beautiful word—a little prayer word—will fill him with music and will lead him into victory.

Learn to make words work for you. Learn to fill words with power that cannot be resisted. The way you fill words with power that cannot be resisted is to fill words with love and faith.

Parents need to realize that the home atmosphere is a product of WORDS.

In 1958, as my wife and I were driving near Los Angeles, she suggested, "Why don't we stop and see Brother and Sister So-and-So?" We had held them a revival several months before, and their house was only about three blocks off the freeway.

"All right," I said, "we'll drive by."

We pulled up in the driveway, but we didn't see any activity. I rang the doorbell. I heard someone coming. The pastor opened the door, shook hands with me, and I motioned for my wife to come inside.

The pastor said, "Brother Hagin, we were resting. My wife will have to dress. Just sit here, in the living room." He had his robe on, so he went off to dress, too. My wife came inside. She didn't see or speak to him.

The moment we sat on that couch, we turned to one another and said at the same time, "Sharp words were spoken in this home!"

The atmosphere was bad. We both sensed it immediately. Spiritual things are created by WORDS. Even natural, physical things are created by WORDS.

If you went into a room where they had just been frying fish, you could smell the fish. It would still be in the atmosphere. The air was heavy in that room. Those WORDS were still in the air. (There are WORDS in the air around you right now. If you don't believe it, turn on a transistor radio.) As we talked to this pastor and his wife, we learned that they had indeed had a disagreement.

The lives and personalities of children brought up in that kind of an atmosphere will be warped. Mothers and Dads: Your home atmosphere is the product of WORDS. Children fail because wrong WORDS were spoken. The right WORDS were not spoken.

Why is it that some families grow up strong, and win life's fight? It's because the right kind of WORDS were spoken in the home.

My wife and I were visiting in New Mexico once on our day off. We drove more than 100 miles to see friends who had just built a beautiful new church.

As they were showing us the new building, the pastor's wife was chatting with my wife, and she said, "You know, we can't do a thing in the world with our oldest boy. He's almost 17. He won't come to church. He wants to join the Navy, and when he gets 17, we're going to sign for him and let him go just to get rid of him. I guess you know what I'm talking about, though. You've got a teenage boy."

My wife replied, "No, I can't understand. You'd have to knock our boy in the head to keep him out of church, even when he probably should stay home to study."

Why? Because he had been trained that way. The right kind of WORDS were spoken in the home. WORDS make a boy love an education. WORDS bring a boy to church or keep him away. We are a product of WORDS.

You can go to church on Sunday, sit there and look pious if you want to, pray and sing in the choir, and even teach Sunday School. But if you fly off the handle at home, cuss, raise the devil, and fuss, you're going to lose your children. They are not being brought up in a church atmosphere. They are being brought up in a home atmosphere. And that church atmosphere on Sunday is going to affect them very little.

One Sunday morning during the summer of 1943, I was preaching at a church in north-central Texas. My text was Colossians 2:9,10, where it says "ye are complete in him," and my title was "What Is Spirituality?" I have never been brave enough to use that text again.

I asked the question: Where would you go to look for a spiritual person?

Some thought of people in our church who were quick to jump, quick to dance, quick to shout, and they said, "They're spiritual."

I told the congregation, "That's not spirituality. You can't judge spirituality by that."

Somebody else said, "So-and-So is always talking in tongues and is always giving messages in tongues, so he's really spiritual."

I said, "No, no. You can't judge spirituality by that, because God will use any kind of vessel He can. I read where He talked through a donkey one time. That doesn't mean that donkey was spiritual.

"No," I said. "I know that spiritual people do go to church, but I wouldn't even go to church if I were looking for a spiritual person. You know the first place I'd go?"

They all said, "No."

I said, "I'd go to a person's home."

You see, when it comes to religious things, people are two faced. They've got one face they wear on Sunday, and another face they wear another day. I've seen them as a pastor. I've knocked on their doors and heard them whisper, "Put that UP! Put that UP! Put that UP!" There was something they didn't want me to see. And you never heard such scurrying around. I thought they never were going to open the door.

"No," I told that congregation, "I'd just like to become the invisible man; walk through the door, and look and listen." And I said, "People who are spiritual—people who have really got something—live right at home. *And if you don't live right at home, you haven't got anything!*"

A lady in the second pew said, "Oh, my God, that lets me out!" (She later said she thought she had just *thought* it; she didn't realize she had said it out loud.)

It ruined my sermon. Everybody burst out laughing. I fell over the pulpit, laughing. I stopped right there, and I've never tried that sermon again.

Chapter 3
'THE TONGUE OF THE WISE
IS HEALTH'

Did you ever visit the sick? Did you ever listen to them talk? If you do, many times you can find out why they are sick.

Proverbs 12:18 is a wonderful revelation, a marvelous truth: *"There is that speaketh like the piercings of a sword: but the tongue of the wise is health."* You are not going to have health unless you talk health.

Did you ever notice that we are programmed wrong? (I'm talking from the natural standpoint.) We are programmed negatively.

The Bible says, *"Blessed is the man that walketh not in the counsel of the ungodly"* (Ps. 1:1). You do not want to think like the world thinks.

Romans 12:1 says, *"I beseech you therefore, brethren, by the mercies of God, that ye present your bodies a living sacrifice, holy, acceptable unto God, which is your reasonable service."*

Now notice verse 2: *"And be not conformed to this world, but be ye transformed by the renewing of your mind."* God does not want you to be conformed to this world, but to be transformed. How? By the renewing of your mind. Do not think like the world thinks. They think negatively.

We have read Romans 12:2, however, and thought it was saying, "Don't do a lot of things that people in the world do." Well, there are a lot of things you do that they do. You eat like they eat, usually, and sleep like they sleep.

Several years ago, I was holding a meeting in a certain church in Oklahoma. They thought women were going to hell unless they had long sleeves, long dresses, long hair—and long tongues. (I added the last part. They put in the first part.) They always talked about "worldliness."

"We're not conformed to the world," they said. "The Bible said 'be not conformed.' We're not worldly."

The pastor asked me to preach on Sunday morning. Every time I woke up Saturday night, I was praying about the message. "God, I don't preach this way ordinarily," I said as I saw what the sermon was to be. But God really dealt with me.

That morning I jumped off the platform, ran up and down the aisles, and said, "I'll tell you, this is the most *worldly* church I've ever preached in!"

It was as if I had slapped them in the face with a wet dishrag! Here I was saying this was the most *worldly* church I was ever in—and they were bragging about how *holy* they were!

They were like the Pharisees. They prayed, "Lord, we're better than anyone else in town. We're just the greatest and the best. We're the most wonderful people. Of course, *we* know that *You* know that. We don't do this; we don't do that; we don't do something else." But they were the most negative bunch I had ever seen.

I said, "You still think just like the world. You think sickness. You think fear. You think doubt. You think defeat. You think failure—

just like the world thinks! Get your mind renewed with the Word of God! *Think* in line with God's Word! *Talk* in line with God's Word! *Believe* in line with God's Word!"

Many people who think they are so separated from the world are sometimes the most worldly people of all. As I said, the whole world is programmed negatively, and if you are not careful, you will make the same mistake the world does. You see, the world without God is in spiritual death. They are programmed to death instead of life.

If a person is frightened, he will say, "That just scares me *to death*. I'm scared to death."

Never say that. I never say I am scared, because I am not.

If I am tempted to be fearful, I speak to it. I say, "Fear, I resist you in Jesus' Name!" I refuse to fear. If doubt comes, I speak to it. I say, "Doubt, I resist you in Jesus' Name!" I refuse to doubt.

I wouldn't tell anybody if I had a doubt-thought, or a fear-thought. I wouldn't accept it. I wouldn't tell somebody if the thought came to me—and you know the devil can put all kinds of thoughts in your mind.

We are a product of WORDS. Did you ever stop to think that the Bible teaches that there is health and healing in your tongue? Did you notice that He said here, *"the tongue of the wise is health"*?

I never talk sickness. I don't believe in sickness. I talk health. *The tongue of the wise is health.* The Bible does not say, "The tongue of the wise is sickness." It says, *"The tongue of the wise is HEALTH."*

I talk health. I believe in healing. I believe in health. I never talk sickness. I never talk disease. I talk health. I talk healing.

I never talk failure. I don't believe in failure. I believe in success. I never talk defeat. I don't believe in defeat. I believe in winning, hallelujah to Jesus!

I never talk about what the devil has done. I'm not interested in his works. I talk about the works of God and what He is doing, praise the Lord! I don't talk about the devil's power, because he is not so powerful as God.

The other night, a preacher on TV spent his whole time talking about what the devil's doing. I thought to myself, *Dear Lord, I'm going to turn that off!* And I turned it off right in the middle of his expose of ignorance. The longer he talked, the worse I felt. He never told anybody anything they didn't already know, and besides that, he was bragging on the devil.

You'd have thought poor old God's gone out of business—lost all His power—and all Christians are going to have to go through life with their noses to the grindstone, sick and afflicted; live on Barely-Get-Along Street, 'way down at the end of the block, right next to Grumble Alley; and sing "If I can just make it in." No victory, no success.

Jesus said, *"I will be with you always"* (Matt. 28:20). I believe if He is with me, that's success.

The Bible says in Romans 8:31, *"If God be for us, who can be against us?"* Oh, glory to God, if He is for us, what difference does it make who's against us? What difference does it make what the devil's doing out in the world? God is for us! He is on our side!

In First John 4:4 it says, *"Greater is he that is in you, than he that is in the world."* What do you care what you face if the GREATER ONE is in you?

I've been tempted to worry, just like everybody else, but I don't worry. I never talk discouragement. I never talk worry. I never talk defeat.

Some people get delivered from smoking cigarettes, and some people get delivered from drinking whiskey, but I wish Christian people would get delivered from the biggest sin—a sin greater than smoking cigarettes or drinking whiskey—the sin of worry.

A lot of people are so proud. They say, "I don't smoke. God delivered me from that." Well, I wish they would be delivered from that big sin they have in their life. The sin of worry is worse than smoking a cigarette.

Smoking and drinking are wrong. I am not in favor of either of them, and I don't have either of those bad habits, but worry is worse than either of them.

Worry will kill you. More than one doctor has said to me (and I've read it in periodicals), "There are more people in mental institutions, and there are more people in the grave because of worry than any other one thing."

What do people worry about? Circumstances. They worry about tomorrow. They worry about the things they face.

I've been tempted to worry about tomorrow and about things I knew I faced. But then I remembered what the Bible said is inside of me. I didn't even have to pray about it. I just looked trouble and seeming impossibilities in the face, and I couldn't help from laughing, praise God.

I said, "If I don't make it over you, I'll make it around you. If I don't make it around you, I'll make it under you. If I don't make it under you, I'll make it through you, because THE GREATER ONE IS IN ME."

And, you know, while I was laughing, that circumstance went off and hid!

THE GREATER ONE IS IN ME. THE GREATER ONE IS IN ME. *GREATER IS HE THAT IS IN YOU, THAN HE THAT IS IN THE WORLD.* Well, who is in the world? The devil is the god of this world. What else is in the world? Sin is, but the GREATER ONE is in me. He's greater than sin. He conquered sin. He put away sin.

What else is in the world? Sickness is in the

world. It's not of God. It doesn't come from heaven. There's no sickness up there; it's of this world. There won't be any sickness in heaven. The GREATER ONE is in me. He's greater than sickness, because He's the healer.

What else is in the world? Trouble is in the world. People are always talking about the trouble that's in this old world. But He that is in me is greater than the trouble that's in the world.

What else is in the world? Adverse circumstances are in the world. Seeming impossibilities are in the world. But I'm not of the world. I may be in the world, but I'm not of the world. My citizenship is in heaven, glory to God! And while I'm down here in the world, I have the GREATER ONE living in me. He is greater than he that is in the world. He will put me over. He will make me a success. Hallelujah, I cannot be defeated.

That's my confession. WORDS. Those are the kinds of words that I have been talking for 40-some years. WORDS. WORDS. WORDS.

Chapter 4
WHAT IS YOUR CONFESSION?

PROVERBS 18:21
21 Death and life are in the power of the tongue:
and they that love it shall eat the fruit thereof.

PROVERBS 21:23
23 Whoso keepeth his mouth and his tongue
keepeth his soul from troubles.

MATTHEW 12:37
37 For by thy words thou shalt be justified, and
by thy words thou shalt be condemned.

MARK 11:23
23 For verily I say unto you, That whosoever
shall say unto this mountain, Be thou removed,
and be thou cast into the sea; and shall not doubt

in his heart, but shall believe that those things which he saith shall come to pass; he shall have whatsoever he saith.

For years faith has been taught in the church. People have been encouraged to believe. But we have not heard much teaching about WORDS, or **saying what you believe.**

The Scripture verses above illustrate the importance of WORDS. Another such verse is Hebrews 4:14, *"Seeing then that we have a great high priest, that is passed into the heavens, Jesus the Son of God, let us hold fast our profession."*

The word translated "profession" in the King James is the same Greek word translated "confession" elsewhere.

In the margin of my Bible opposite this verse is the note "in the Greek, *confession*." I looked up this word in the Greek concordance, read other translations, and found that the Greek text actually says, *"Let us hold fast to saying the same thing."*

Notice again that WORDS are involved.

More than 40 years ago, as a Baptist boy on a bed of sickness, I began to understand Mark

11:23, *"whosoever shall say . . . and shall not
doubt in his heart, but shall believe that those
things which he saith shall come to pass; he
shall have whatsoever he saith."* In other words,
he will have THE WORDS he speaks.

Born and reared a Southern Baptist, I was
taught to believe for salvation and to believe
the Bible. When I saw these truths in Mark
11:23, I believed them. The thing that had kept
me bedfast for 16 months was not knowing how
to turn my faith loose.

You won't get the blessings of God just
because you have faith. You won't get healed or
baptized in the Holy Spirit just because you
have faith. You won't get answers to prayer just
because you have faith. Most Christians think
they will, but they are wrong. The Bible does
not teach it.

The Bible teaches that you get saved
because you believe *and say something—*
not just because you believe.

ROMANS 10:9,10
**9 That if thou shalt confess with thy mouth the
Lord Jesus, and shall believe in thine heart that
God hath raised him from the dead, thou shalt**

be saved.

10 For with the heart man believeth unto right-
eousness; and with the mouth confession is
made unto salvation.

Not only does your heart have something to
do with your salvation, your *mouth* has
something to do with it, too. WORDS have
something to do with it.

The Bible does not say simply that if you
believe in your heart that God raised Jesus
from the dead, you will be saved. You will not be
saved just because you believe it. Notice in the
10th verse the phrase "*with the mouth.*" *With
the mouth* confession is made unto salvation.

MARK 11:23

23 ... whosoever ... shall not doubt in his
heart, but shall believe that those things which
he saith shall come to pass; he shall have
whatsoever he saith.

Jesus did not teach in Mark 11:23, "he shall
have whatsoever he *believeth.*" He taught, "he
shall have whatsoever he *saith.*" In other
words, you will have what you speak. You will
have your WORDS.

Faith is always expressed in WORDS. Faith must be released in WORDS *through your mouth.* We can see that in all of these Scriptures we have read. When you *speak* something, that is *action.* It took me a long time to discover that—16 months of being bedfast—because nobody had ever taught me that.

I'm not talking about the WORDS you speak in church, or the WORDS you use when you pray. I'm talking about the WORDS you use in your everyday life: the WORDS you speak at home, with your friends, at work. These everyday WORDS do three things *to* you and *for* you:

1. The WORDS you speak identify you.
2. The Words you speak set the boundaries of your life.
3. The WORDS you speak affect your spirit (your inward man).

If you want to locate yourself, just listen to the WORDS you speak.

You'll never realize beyond your WORDS. To put it another way, Jesus said in Mark 11:23, *"he shall have whatsoever he saith."*

The thing that defeats a lot of people is their double confession. One time they will confess one thing, and the next time they will confess something else.

If you talk to them, they will say, "Yes, the Lord is my shepherd; I shall not want. Yes, I know that it says in Philippians 4:19, *'My God shall supply all your need according to his riches in glory by Christ Jesus,'* and I'm believing God to supply my needs."

But then they will see somebody down the block, in the store, or at church. They will have their mind on their problems, and they will say, "Well, we're not doing too well. We're so far behind in our bills, we're about to lose our car and everything."

What about that other confession? This second confession nullified the first.

Learn to say the same thing. In Greek, Hebrews 4:14 literally says, *"Let us hold fast to saying the same thing."*

Never, never give up. No, it's not easy. If you're looking for something easy, you might as well give up and crawl in your hole and die. You're not worth a thing.

32

The Bible said, "fight." I think that's as far as some people read. They started fighting. They thought that meant fight other churches, or fellow Christians. No, that's not what it said in 1 Timothy 6:12. You're supposed to fight "the good fight of faith."

In this fight, you've got to fight all of your physical senses. Sometimes you've got to fight what all of your relatives say. Sometimes you've got to fight what the pastor says. Sometimes you've got to fight what all the church members say. Sometimes you've got to fight what a Sunday School teacher says. I know. I've been there.

There were times I made a confession and ignored everybody. It was a fight to do it, because they were all telling me I was wrong and it wouldn't work. It did work; it does work.

Too many people are looking for somebody to do something for them. I can't fight your fight, and you can't fight my fight. You'll have to fight your own fight.

Your WORDS are so important. You need to realize that. They set the boundaries of your life. **You will never realize anything beyond the words you speak. You will never have anything beyond your own words.**